Original title:
Sunspot Speeches

Copyright © 2025 Creative Arts Management OÜ
All rights reserved.

Author: Evelyn Hartman
ISBN HARDBACK: 978-1-80567-861-8
ISBN PAPERBACK: 978-1-80567-982-0

The Warmth of Words

Words dance like fireflies, bright in the gloom,
Chasing shadows with laughter, filling the room.
Tickling ears with tales that bubble and burst,
Every giggle and snort, oh how they thirst!

They hug like a blanket, bringing cheer around,
In the garden of banter, joy is profound.
Like puppies in puddles, they leap and they bound,
Words weave silly spells, in hilarity drowned.

Flashes of Intention

Bright bursts of humor flicker and tease,
Jokes soar like kites on a sunny breeze.
Punchlines erupt like fireworks at night,
Leaving smiles in their wake, oh what a sight!

Each wink is a wink, each nudge a delight,
Chasing off gloom like a kite in flight.
Mirth in the air, a contagious embrace,
Flashes of fun, all silly and chaste.

Spectrum of Silence

In the quietest corners, giggles reside,
Whispers of warmth that no one can hide.
A snicker, a chuckle, muffled and sly,
Creating a canvas where laughter can fly.

Silence can shimmer with glimmers of glee,
Just waiting to burst, like a bee in a spree.
When calm meets the silly, it frolics and plays,
A spectrum of joy in the most subtle ways.

Light's Love Letters

Notes scrawled in sunshine, bright and absurd,
Tales spun with humor, all beautifully blurred.
Each line is a tickle, a wink in disguise,
Whispers of warmth that dance in our eyes.

Letters wrapped in laughter, sealed with a grin,
A treasure of jest that we all hold within.
Messages glimmer like stars in the sky,
Light-hearted confessions that make spirits fly.

Burst of Radiance

A glow in the sky, so bright and dandy,
It tickles the stars, oh isn't that handy?
With spots like a leopard, it dances and twirls,
Making the cosmos laugh, as it swirls and unfurls.

When it speaks, it sounds like a giggling ray,
Chasing away shadows, come join in the play!
Its words are like bubbles, all bouncing around,
A frolicsome banter, in laughter, we're bound.

Stellar Rhetoric

In a conference of orbs, bright and merry,
One shoots its ideas like ripe, juicy cherry!
With a wink and a nod, it shares with delight,
Tales of the cosmos, oh what a sight!

Each twinkle a word, a whimsical jest,
Gravity laughing, it's time to invest!
A cosmic comedian, high in the sky,
With punchlines so bright, the universe sighs.

Photon Footprints

Each little shimmer leaves tracks in the night,
Dancing like children, all filled up with light!
They giggle and skip, these beams on the run,
   Creating a trail of mischief and fun!

In every bright glint, there's laughter to share,
   Photon footprints giggle, floating in air.
Chasing away gloom, with a wink and a grin,
   As laughter erupts in the vastness within.

Glimmers of Insight

When wisdom arrives with a sparkle and shine,
It tickles the brain—oh isn't it fine?
With a chortle so bright, it sprouts up like grass,
In the fields of our thoughts, it's a merry, bold class!

Each glimmer a joke, a witty little tease,
Bubbling with joy, like a soft summer breeze.
Lighting our minds, like a robust flare,
Every chuckle a spark, igniting the air!

Vibrant Verbal Visions

Words tumble like chubby bunnies,
With giggles that dance in the air.
Conversations wrapped in honey,
Where puns grow legs and dare.

Rhymes leap like frogs on a spree,
Tickling your soul with delight.
Each line is as bouncy as can be,
Bringing nonsense into the light.

Caresses of Color

Brush strokes of talk paint the room,
With jokes that shine brighter than gold.
Metaphors twirl, and laughter blooms,
Each quip a treasure, a story told.

Swirls of giggles float in the breeze,
As witticisms dance on the tongue.
Colors of laughter aim to please,
In a symphony gaily sung.

Paths of Illumination

Light beams of wit bounce 'round like balls,
   With quips that ignite the dull night.
We stroll through corridors lined with calls,
   Joking shadows that giggle in flight.

Each corner we turn is absurdly bright,
   With phrases that jump over fences.
Our chatter, a dazzling delight,
   Creating a world full of senses.

Discourse in the Dawnlight

Morning whispers tickle our ears,
As banter wakes up the sleepy sun.
We juggle our thoughts with no fears,
Making laughter the ultimate fun.

Chasing the day with silly retorts,
As shadows start to stretch and bend.
Together we create our own courts,
Where playfulness knows no end.

Twilight Tales

In the dusk, the shadows dance,
A cat declares a silly prance.
The moon's a cheese, so bright and round,
While tumbleweeds just roll around.

A turtle dons a tie to chat,
While squirrels plot to steal the hat.
They laugh and joke, no worries found,
In twilight's glow, they're glory-bound.

Radiant Resonance

A lamp once wished upon a star,
To glow brighter than a car.
It flickered, flattered by the praise,
And now it shines in silly ways.

The toaster wants to be a star,
But burns the bread, oh, how bizarre!
With jam as props, it starts a show,
But crumbs land everywhere, oh no!

Spectrum of Sentiments

Colors clash in a silly spree,
A rainbow bursts with glee, you see.
The reds and blues begin to wink,
While yellows giggle—what a link!

A purple cat juggles the hues,
While dancing happily in shoes.
The greens just grumble, 'What is this?'
But join in on the vibrant bliss!

Illuminated Insights

A light bulb gleams, a thinker's dream,
Yet often goes dim from the team.
With brainstorms swirling, all a mess,
It laughs, 'Hey, I'm the brightest - yes!'

A candle snickers, 'Let me shine,
For wisdom lights in silly line!'
With quirks and quirks, they chat away,
Illuminating thoughts in play.

Golden Soliloquies

In a world where suns might play,
We roast our thoughts in golden rays.
Shiny ideas bounce about,
Making us laugh, that's what it's about.

A solar flare with witty sparks,
Tickles our minds and warms our hearts.
We joke about the heat today,
While shadows dance in a funny way.

Giggles bounce in loops of light,
Ideas twist and twirl in sight.
Like sunbeams prancing, full of cheer,
These golden moments draw us near.

A burst of laughter, bright and bold,
Turning mundane thoughts to gold.
With every chuckle, every jest,
We find the humor in this quest.

Blazing Discourse

When brilliance flares and jokes ignite,
We gather 'round, all spirits bright.
A fiery talk with loads of laughs,
As witty banter gently drafts.

The heat is on, and puns are great,
Timely quips we celebrate.
Who knew such warmth could be so fun,
With phrases sizzled in the sun?

Words leap like flames, they dance and spin,
Tickling thoughts, igniting grins.
Amidst this blaze, we share our tales,
As laughter flows like summer gales.

In blazing chatter, we'll not tire,
Each punchline's spark becomes a fire.
Together we bask in warmth and cheer,
Turning fleeting moments into the dear.

Photon Perspectives

From photons bouncing in free flight,
We gather maps of joy and light.
A spectrum of laughter, wide and free,
Painting tales of pure glee.

Oh, how the wavelengths twist and twirl,
In this bright world, our stories swirl.
Each beam a joke, each hue a jest,
In vibrant talks, we feel our best.

Let's shift dimensions, dance and spin,
With ideas that laugh and brightly grin.
In this playful realm where light does bend,
We chase the giggles that never end.

Turning notions into playful beams,
Pouring out laughter like fun-filled dreams.
Photon perspectives guide our way,
In this whimsical light ballet.

Spectrum of Voices

In a spectrum where colors collide,
Voices sparkle, each with pride.
From reds to blues, a funny scheme,
We share our thoughts like a vivid dream.

With every tone, a chuckle grows,
As laughter paints the air with prose.
Hues of humor we deftly blend,
In a chorus of joy that knows no end.

Each shade a story, bright and bold,
Through laughter's lens, we're never cold.
In this array of clever quips,
We ride the waves of silly trips.

Voices mingle in a playful sound,
As we spin tales, round and round.
Spectrum of giggles, what a grand show,
In this joyful blending, we all glow.

Messages on the Breeze

A cloud of chatter, floating wide,
With secrets swirling where they hide.
The wind can carry tales so bright,
Like giggles trapped in morning light.

Silly whispers start to race,
Dancing lightly, losing space.
Each gust a jest, a playful tease,
As laughter tumbles through the trees.

Messages from skies that play,
Like children's laughter on a sunny day.
They tickle ears and spin around,
These breezy words, a frolic found.

So let them swirl, let them fly,
With quirky rhymes that float on by.
In every gust, a giggle lives,
A joyful chorus that nature gives.

Solar Tales Untold

Once upon a beam of light,
A shadow danced, oh what a sight!
It flipped and flopped upon the floor,
And giggled softly, wanting more.

Each ray that hit the cheeky sun,
Would wink and twirl, oh what fun!
They twinkled tales of days gone by,
Of silly quirks and birds that fly.

A sunbeam spoke of ice cream dreams,
Of goofy hats and funny schemes.
With humor wrapped up in its glow,
It shared a jest, then let it go.

So listen close to solar games,
Where light and laughter call your name.
In every beam, a smile's spun,
A funny tale for everyone.

Whispered Brightness

In a sunbeam's soft embrace,
Bright whispers dart, a light-filled race.
They tickle thoughts and spark delight,
With jokes as sweet as candy bites.

A photon's chuckle, quick and sly,
Zips past the clouds, oh my, oh my!
It weaves through trees, a sneaky grin,
As morning giggles tiptoe in.

Bright whispers flutter, tickling ears,
A melody that drowns out fears.
They dance in eddies, laugh in cheer,
With every twinkle, they draw near.

For in each ray of golden hue,
Are funny tales just made for you.
A whispered jest, a wink in light,
Brings warmth and laughter, pure delight.

Expressions in Gold

Expressions shine in colors loud,
Like silly hats upon a crowd.
Golden rays in a playful mood,
Invite us all to laugh and brood.

Each glint of light, a quirky face,
With chuckles that we can embrace.
They wiggle, jiggle, swirl with glee,
As sunbeams paint their symphony.

The horizon sparkles, joins the fun,
As colors drip from evening sun.
They flaunt bright smiles, all aglow,
Turning frowns to art, don't you know?

So raise your voice, let laughter roll,
In gold expressions, hand in soul.
The sun has tales just waiting there,
For joy and humor, if you dare!

Glistening Narratives

In the sky, a sparkle bright,
Tales of golden light take flight.
Witty whispers drifting high,
As giggles twinkle in the sky.

A comet's wink, a moonlight grin,
The stars join in the jovial spin.
Cosmic pranks and radiant laughs,
Drawing smiles in sunny drafts.

Jests from planets, oh what a tease,
Asteroids prance with such great ease.
Giggles echo across the night,
A universe of pure delight.

Join the fun in this vast expanse,
Celestial bodies in a dance.
With each twinkle, a cheeky cheer,
Laughing loudly, far and near.

Horizon Hues and Hues

Where colors blend and laughter blooms,
A palette filled with joyful tunes.
Horizon lines with silly spins,
Where every shade reveals a grin.

Pastel whispers, bold and bright,
Painting dreams in morning light.
Each hue tells a funny tale,
From violet giggles to orange wail.

Yellow chuckles, red delights,
Swirling in the playful nights.
A canvas vast, our laughter fused,
With every stroke, life is amused.

In this world, so full of cheer,
Colors dance, and jokes appear.
A horizon dipped in silly ways,
Basking in the bright sun's rays.

Lightwaves of Expression

Rippling rays with humor bright,
Dance around with sheer delight.
Funny flashes, oh so clear,
Each wave brings a joyful cheer.

Giggles float on beams of gold,
Stories spun, hilariously told.
In the ether, laughter soars,
Filling hearts and opening doors.

Light dashes and playful beams,
Like sparks igniting all our dreams.
We ride the waves of happiness,
In this shimmer, we are blessed.

So catch a wave, don't be late,
Join the fun before it's fate.
With light as our muse, we will create,
A world where laughter resonates.

Flares of Thought

Bursting ideas that dance and flare,
Silly wisdom beyond compare.
Thoughts ignite in vibrant hues,
A sparky mix of me and you.

How many giggles can we share?
In every burst, a hearty dare.
With every flare, let laughter grow,
In this fire light, our spirits glow.

Witty sparks that light the night,
With humor wrapped in sheer delight.
Flares of thought, our minds release,
In this chaos, we find peace.

So come along, let's light the way,
With flares of thought, we'll laugh and play.
Each burst a treasure, full of jest,
In the glow of laughter, we are blessed.

Timeless Radiance

In the sky, a flicker plays,
Stretched shadows in a sunny haze.
A squirrel tries to mime, you see,
With acorns as his props, how free!

Grinning rays take on a tone,
As clouds stick out their tongue, they moan.
Why do you frown when bright is near?
Get ready for a giggle, my dear!

Light dances, swaying in delight,
A butterfly joins in the flight.
Tickled petals whisper tales,
Of breeze-blown dreams and happy trails.

The sun, a joker, shines so bold,
With warmth like stories often told.
So, laugh along under the glow,
For fun is what the bright can sow!

Stories in Sunshine

Once there was a sunbeam bright,
Who tickled trees with pure delight.
It told a tale with golden grace,
Crafting smiles on every face.

The daisies twirled in pure delight,
Chatting 'bout clouds in the warm sunlight.
A bee buzzed by with a pun or two,
Sipping nectar, just passing through.

Old Mr. Moon felt quite left out,
So, he yelled, 'Hey! Watch me shout!'
But the sun just winked and laughed all day,
While the moon hung back to fade away.

With every ray, a giggle flies,
Stories told beneath blue skies.
A joyful chorus, bright and keen,
In sunshine laughter, all is seen!

Celestial Chronicles

A comet sneezed, what a surprise!
Scattered stars fell from the skies.
Jupiter chuckled, spinning round,
As cosmic laughter knew no bound.

A wink from Mars, a twirl on cue,
Saturn's rings danced in the view.
Galaxies giggled far and wide,
In the universe, no need to hide.

Planets trade tales on cosmic trips,
With comets and asteroids sharing quips.
'Why did the star feel so alone?'
'Because it couldn't find its home zone!'

The sun blushed in hues of ochre,
As laughter shimmered like sweet mocha.
So, let's embrace the cosmic jest,
In this vast sky, we are all blessed!

Illuminated Conversations

In a café made of rays and light,
The sun sipped coffee, feeling bright.
'What's on the menu today, my friend?'
'Extra joy, with laughter to blend!'

Clouds served whispers, fluffy and cool,
While shadows danced, creating a pool.
The sun cracked jokes, jokes about time,
As moonbeams chuckled, keeping in rhyme.

With every sip, the sunlight sighed,
'We're all just glowing, can't be denied!'
Stars chimed in, echoing glee,
In this café of pure jubilee.

So come and join the radiant cheer,
Where fun is served, never a fear.
With bright conversations that shine all day,
In these moments, we all can play!

Conversations with the Cosmos

I asked the stars for some advice,
They winked and giggled, oh so nice.
"Your worries are as big as space,"
"Just float around, find a new place."

My phone buzzed, with cosmic text,
"The moon's on hold, do not be vexed."
A shooting star made quite a fuss,
"Your dreams are safe, just ride the bus!"

Neptune laughed, said, "What a joke!"
"Light-years away, but I still poke."
The sun just yawned, then took a nap,
While comets drifted in natty chap."

Then echoes of laughter filled the night,
Galaxies twinkled, what a sight!
In this universe of quirk and twist,
We found our joy, who needs a list?

Heat-Hued Insights

The sun told me a tall, tall tale,
Of warming skies and ships to sail.
"Life's just a sunbeam running free,"
"With giggles sprinkled, just like me!"

In funky colors, the planets danced,
While asteroids took a chance, entrance.
"Fire's not hot, it's just a craze,"
"Get too close, you'll get a blaze!"

Venus chimed with a zany grin,
"Why take a bath? Just let it spin!"
And Mars jumped in, oh such a clown,
Turning red with laughter, upside down!

With quirky quirks, each star sighs,
The universe cracks jokes in the skies.
From orbits wide to a comet's flight,
Every twinkle glimmers with delight!

Luminous Legacy

A comet's tail is quite a sight,
It's like a joke that's light and bright.
"Catch it quick, before it's gone!"
"Turn up your laugh, let joy dawn!"

The nebula giggled with each hue,
Sprinkling stardust like morning dew.
"Why worry much about your fate?"
"Just grab a snack; it's never too late!"

Galaxies clash, but it's all in fun,
They spin and twirl, oh what a run!
"Dance your worries away with glee,"
"In the cosmic show, it's all for free!"

Memories made in starry flight,
Leave a legacy of sheer delight.
So dance with the cosmos, make a scene,
Laugh with the lights, and keep it clean!

Chasing Light's Echo

I chased a photon down the lane,
It giggled back, what a silly game!
"Catch me if you can, it's all a tease,"
"Just follow the path through cosmic breeze!"

Light beams twinkled in playful jest,
While shadows lurked, giving their best.
"Don't let them fool you, just step bright,"
"Keep your heart light, enjoy the flight!"

Reflections winked in the dark night,
Whispering secrets of pure delight.
"Echoes of laughter bounce around,
Even in silence, joy can be found!"

So here's to chasing each bright refrain,
With cosmic humor and sunshine's gain.
In this chase, may you always find,
That laughter's the spark that leaves us aligned!

Glimmering Parleys

In the shade, we chat and jest,
With laughs that bubble like a jest.
Words twinkle like stars on a whim,
As we dance on sunlight's limb.

Jokes fly like rays in the breeze,
Brightening faces, putting minds at ease.
Oh, the chortles, how they gleam,
Crafted in a shimmering dream.

Chasing shadows of silly pranks,
Our thoughts light up in joyful ranks.
In every chuckle, a spark ignites,
Creating scenes of silly delights.

So gather 'round, let laughter ring,
In the glow of this radiant spring.
For in each word, there's a twinkling flame,
In every parley, fun's the game.

Radiance in Rhetoric

Words are dancing, bright and bold,
In quirky tales, our stories unfold.
Each sentence sparkles with playful charm,
As we weave magic with laughter's balm.

Like sunshine breaking through a cloud,
Our jokes assemble a merry crowd.
A pun here, a pun there, they gleefully fly,
With giggles that bounce and soar high.

In this arena of radiant wit,
We trade quips, never to quit.
Ideas shine like comedies bright,
Twisting and turning, oh what a sight!

So let's toast to the joy we craft,
With words, we draw smiles and a laugh.
In this dance of rhetoric divine,
We embrace the fun, one pun at a time.

Solar Whispers

Whispers float like dandelion seeds,
Carrying tales of cheeky deeds.
In the warmth of light, we conspire,
With giggles rising higher and higher.

Charming secrets drift through the air,
Laughter dancing without a care.
Every chuckle is a little ray,
In the portrait of our sunny play.

Jests secretly sail on gentle breeze,
Tickling minds with playful tease.
In every glimmer, a story shines,
As we share our quirks, crossing lines.

Let the world catch our sparkle bright,
With whispers of joy weaving through the night.
Together we bask in friendly cheer,
Creating memories year after year.

Celestial Conversations

Stars twinkle as we share our tales,
With laughter soaring like comet trails.
In the cosmos, we roast and rhyme,
Finding humor amidst the time.

Chitchat glimmers like astral light,
Turning mundane to sheer delight.
With every quip, a starlight dance,
In this galactic, comic romance.

So spin those yarns, let the fun unfold,
As we barter laughs, both young and old.
In celestial realms, we shine and play,
Creating moments that always stay.

Thus we gather in this radiant spree,
Laughing under our cosmic marquee.
In our universe of jests and cheer,
Every conversation, a treasure dear.

Ethereal Eloquence

A comet danced on the moon,
Made jokes with stars in June.
The planets laughed in their orbits tight,
As comets shared tales of cosmic light.

Galaxies spun, a swirling joke,
Even black holes had a funny poke.
They said, 'What's the best way to shine?'
'Just laugh, my friend, and you'll do fine!'

From nebulae bright came a roaring sound,
As cosmic jesters played all around.
They twinkled with glee, lighting the night,
In an ether of laughter, oh what a sight!

So let's toast to humor in the skies,
With giggles and chuckles as our prize.
For laughter's the language of stars so bright,
In a universe glowing, full of delight!

Shine and Discourse

A glimmer spoke to a gleam one day,
'Tell me, dear friend, how do you play?'
The shine responded with a twinkling chime,
'I sprinkle laughter in rhythm and rhyme!'

They gathered the photons, made them all cheer,
With jokes about gravity that drew them near.
Witty remarks flew with joy in the air,
As radiant giggles were found everywhere.

A dazzling spark said, 'What's in a beam?'
'Just light and laughter, or so it would seem!'
And thus they danced in a radiant show,
Where light-hearted chatter began to flow.

So join in the fun under cosmic skies,
With luminous laughter as our prize.
For in this bright banter, we find our way,
With shine and discourse brightening the day!

Sunbeam Soliloquies

A sunbeam whispered to a cloud so fluffy,
'Why so serious? You look all huffy!'
The cloud chuckled, 'I'm just up here,
Waiting for raindrops, bring some cheer.'

The sunbeam giggled, 'Let's lighten the mood,
With jests so bright, we'll banish the brood!'
They tossed out puns that sparkled with glee,
As shadows danced with a lighthearted spree.

The horizon blushed with a golden draw,
As beams and clouds crafted their whimsical law.
'There's nothing weighty about being light,
Comedic sunshine, that's our delight!'

So here's to the brightness that banters and beams,
Crafting tales away from the mundane themes.
In the world of laughter, we find our goal,
With sunbeam soliloquies, we dance and stroll!

Bright Insights

A bright light bulb had an idea so grand,
'Tell me, dear friend, can you lend me a hand?'
The shadow replied with a knowing grin,
'Surely, but only if we can begin!'

They brainstormed jokes about things that shine,
Like disco balls spinning, oh isn't that fine?
With giggly thoughts that lit up the night,
Whimsical wisdom, oh what a sight!

'Why did the star refuse to play?
Because it felt dim and lost its way!'
They laughed until the dawn brought its light,
Sharing bright insights, oh what a delight!

So come share a chuckle when darkness falls,
In the glow of laughter, the universe calls.
For bright insights bring joy to our days,
As we dance in the light of our whimsical ways!

Sunlit Orations

When the sun starts to flicker and dance,
I give my best joke a chance.
The photons giggle, they can't contain,
Radiant laughter, a bright refrain.

With rays that glimmer and wink so bright,
My words take flight like sprites in the light.
They bounce off clouds, they run and play,
Join in the fun, come out and stay.

Jokes about shadows, so silly and spry,
Even the birds stop by to sigh.
My audience warms under heavenly beams,
Collective chuckles, a sunlit dream.

As dusk approaches, we split our sides,
Chasing the sun where the humor resides.
Each parting word carries warmth and cheer,
Goodbye for now, but don't you fear!

Chromatic Exchanges

Colors clash in a vibrant debate,
Green with envy, while yellow just waits.
The reds joke loudly, the blues pout and sigh,
In the spectrum of smiles, no one's shy.

Polka dot norms start to shake and sway,
Purple proposes a whimsical way.
While orange slips in with a snarky grin,
"Who's got the puns? Let's all begin!"

The palette erupts, a visual feast,
Jokes about rainbows, they never cease.
Laughter paints the air with brilliant rays,
Splashes of joy in zany displays.

As the hues dissolve into twilight's glow,
Our colorful tales keep ebbing and flow.
In every shade, the humor blends tight,
Echoing joy as day turns to night.

Solar Flare Reflections

A flare erupts, a cosmic delight,
Jokes about planets take charming flight.
Mercury grins, what a speedy chap,
Venus giggles, caught in a trap.

Saturn's rings twirl in comedic jest,
While Jupiter's dance is simply the best.
Mars throws a quip, so dry and witty,
Earth rolls its eyes, isn't it pretty?

As solar winds whisk our laughs away,
Each planetary pun makes brighter the day.
In the vastness, we find common ground,
Amongst the stars, our laughter is found.

So here we are, embracing the glow,
With cosmic charm in the ebb and flow.
Even in space, humor takes flight,
It's endless, it sparkles, a pure delight!

Illuminated Rhetoric

In this discourse of dazzling delight,
Words dance like fireflies taking flight.
Illumination's antics are far from mundane,
In the spotlight's warmth, I'll entertain.

Each syllable glimmers, a sparkling blast,
With a quirk here and there, we're having a blast.
The audience chuckles, the critics erupt,
With laughter like beams, we're all swept up.

Bright ideas twinkle like stars in the night,
Witty comparisons, oh what a sight!
The stage is aglow, with warmth in the air,
Connecting us all in this jovial affair.

As the lights start to fade and the laughter subsides,
We'll carry these moments, like glimmering tides.
In the end, what matters is humor shared brief,
With lighthearted words, we find common relief.

Celestial Whimsy

In a galaxy far away,
Stars wear hats made of clay.
The comets giggle, taking flight,
While planets spin in sheer delight.

Saturn serves a cake on a ring,
Jupiter dances, what a thing!
Uranus jokes, it's all a ruse,
As the cosmos bursts with laughs and blues.

Meteorites with ticklish tails,
Play hide and seek in cosmic veils.
A solar flare cracks a joke so bold,
The universe bursts, in laughter, unfolds.

Aliens gather for a cosmic chat,
Wearing shoes shaped like a cat.
They talk of cheese and cosmic dough,
In this patch of sky, a funny show.

Heat of the Moment

When the stars are hot like toast,
The sun beams in, and we all boast.
Planets fan themselves with glee,
As solar rays sip iced tea.

A fiery sun, a sassy glare,
Screams, 'Who stole my solar flare?'
Venus twirls, doing the samba,
While Mars just stands, no big drama.

The sun's a chef, it cooks up storms,
While its rays do silly forms.
A sunburnt smile, laughter's delight,
Heat waves dance through day and night.

The cosmos laughs in a sizzling spree,
As stars unite in harmony.
What fun it is to toast on high,
In this sun-kissed, jolly sky.

Flickering Fantasies

In the twilight, shadows play,
Stars peek out, ready to sway.
Moonbeams whisper jokes at night,
Painting dreams in silver light.

A comet trips on stardust trail,
And giggles echo, we can't fail.
In this realm, where wishes soar,
Time hides laughter behind each door.

Constellations weave a silly tale,
Of a turtle riding on a whale.
Big dipper spins, winks with a laugh,
As stars line up for the photobomb path.

With each twinkle, a story unfolds,
Of forgotten dreams and wishes told.
The universe plays its funny games,
In this dance of cosmic names.

Dialogue in the Dawn

At dawn, the stars start to yawn,
The sun ticks in, like a quirky pawn.
'Hey Night,' it calls, 'you won't believe,
The dreams I've spun, oh, don't deceive.'

Moon chuckles softly, fading away,
'Your puns are bright, but I'm here to stay.'
Light banter fills the morning air,
As sunbeams mess with tousled hair.

Clouds drift by, in laughter's hold,
Whispering secrets, both wise and bold.
They roll in giggles, so light and free,
While pinks and golds paint the jubilee.

The dawn giggles, the world awakes,
In this banter, laughter shakes.
With every ray, a joke is spun,
In this chat, the day has begun.

The Art of Shine

In the glow, we dance and sway,
Those rays just love to play.
Twirling beams on picnic grounds,
Laughter echoes, joy abounds.

The sun, a jokester in disguise,
Peeking through with silly eyes.
It tickles leaves and warms the air,
Spreading giggles everywhere.

A sunbeam tells a joke so bright,
It sparkles with sheer delight.
Let's roast marshmallows, catch some fun,
Under the antics of this sun.

With every wink, it starts the laughs,
As shadows dance in goofy drafts.
Come join the funny parade,
Where sunny moments never fade.

Messages from the Sun

It sends a letter, bright and bold,
In warmest hues, a story told.
'Dear Earthlings, don't take life too serious!'
Smile wide; it's all quite hilarious!

A wacky chatter fills the sky,
Leveling clouds with a cheeky sigh.
"Stay bright; don't let shadows succeed,
Chase after laughter, it's all you need!"

When twilight whispers sweeter tunes,
And stars begin their cartoon poons.
The sun is off, but not away,
It jokes around in a different way.

So gather close, with hearts aglow,
And spread the giggles all we know.
For messages from up above,
Spark joy and laughter, they spread love!

Daylight Confessions

In the morning, a secret peeks,
With every ray, a bright cheek speaks.
"I mischief my way through your day,
Chasing your worries, come what may!"

It confesses with radiant flair,
"I'm here to lighten up your air.
So leave behind your frowny face,
And join this silly sunlit race!"

With sunbeams bouncing in the park,
We giggle till we make a mark.
"Don't be boring, poke some fun,
Life's too short; let's bask and run!"

The daylight chuckles as it fades,
We carry laughter, like parades.
In glowing whispers, tales we share,
With every outing, sunny care.

Cosmic Chatter

Up in space, the sun does shout,
"Hey, Earth! What's this fuss about?"
With cosmic giggles, it beams so wide,
While moon grins, trying to hide!

"Listen up, I'm a star of fun,
Been high and bright since I was spun.
Dancing planets in my rays,
Chasing away your cloudy days!"

Asteroids laugh as they whiz on by,
Comets cracking jokes in the sky.
"Let's toast marshmallows with shooting stars,
And play tag through Venus and Mars!"

So here's to laughter, bright and bold,
In cosmic chatter, stories unfold.
So shine on bright, wherever you roam,
In this universe, you're never alone!

Solar Whispers

Up in the sky, a star so bright,
It cracks a joke in the middle of night.
The planets giggle, they spin in place,
As Luna rolls eyes, at the sun's funny face.

A comet swoops by, trying to dance,
While asteroids laugh, they miss their chance.
"Hey, you missed it!" the Milky Way jokes,
Their laughter echoes, like sunlight pokes.

But Venus just sighs, with a glimmering grin,
"When is this whole cosmic comedy to begin?"
Each star takes a turn, with a pun or two,
Cosmic humor, for me and for you.

And when night is done, and dawn's on the rise,
The universe chuckles, its secrets disguised.
With whispers of joy, the cosmos spins round,
In a ballet of laughter, pure joy can be found.

Celestial Conversations

On a starry night, they gather and talk,
Each celestial body, with its own unique walk.
The sun says, "I'm so bright, can't you see?"
The moon winks back, "You illuminate me!"

"What's round, shiny, and always so bold?"
Asks Mars with a grin, feeling quite told.
"Me!" shouts the sun, with a playful fling,
While Saturn just beckons, and starts to sing.

The asteroids jump in, with cheerful delight,
"We could make music, let's dance through the night!"
But Jupiter's voice rings, so deep and so wide,
"Keep it down, my friends, I need a good hide!"

And as laughter erupts, they twinkle and shine,
In a cosmic café, where stars sip on wine.
With a wink and a giggle, they raise their toast,
To friendship that glows, in the universe ghost.

Radiant Arguments

A solar flare yells, "I'm the hottest in town!"
While Mercury rolls eyes, and lets out a frown.
"Too much heat, you'll melt!" it chimes back with glee,
The sun just chuckles, "Try being me!"

Jupiter boasts with its giant swirl,
"I can spin faster than any girl!"
But Neptune replies, in soft, steady tones,
"Just wait till I launch my ice-cold drones."

Venus pipes up, "Let's not start a fight,
We can all shine brighter, if we just unite!"
While Earth spins around, with a wise, knowing smile,
"Let's parade through the stars, let's enjoy for a while."

And so they all laughed, in this radiant show,
With arguments fading like twilight's soft glow.
In the heart of the cosmos, where wonders impart,
Each spark of joy shines, drawn from the heart.

Luminous Dialogues

Two stars met up for a chat and a cheer,
"Why do you shine so bright, my dear?"
"It's easy," said one, with a twinkle in sight,
"Just borrow some light from the Moon tonight!"

The planets gathered, with tales to share,
Saturn said, "My rings give me flair!"
While Venus flipped hair, with a flirty display,
"Try being this pretty, you'll brighten your day!"

Then came a black hole, with jokes full of spin,
"Got lost in space, but I'm destined to win!"
Galaxies chuckled, jazzing in sync,
"Cosmic confusion? Just sit down and think!"

With laughter erupting in endless delight,
Each celestial being embraced the night.
They danced through the cosmos, engaging in bliss,
In luminous dialogues, how could they miss?

Voices of the Horizon

On the edge where shadows play,
Birds discuss the light of day.
Squirrels joke with the sun's bright glare,
While clouds chuckle, dancing in air.

A bee buzzing, full of flair,
Whispers secrets, oh so rare.
Leaves rustle, giggles in the breeze,
Nature's laughter, a joyful tease.

Raccoons in a playful debate,
Mock the stars, it's quite a fate.
With every laugh, the sky ignites,
A canvas woven with silly sights.

In this realm of giggling rays,
The world shines bright in joyful ways.
A symphony of humor sings,
As each bright moment gently clings.

Afterglow Conversations

When twilight whispers softly low,
Crickets join in, putting on a show.
Fireflies wink, a secret ballet,
Lighting up the night's sweet array.

Mice exchange tales of cheese galore,
While frogs croak jokes from the lily's core.
Waves of laughter crash like the tide,
As stars peep in, shy but wide.

Owls hoot puns from their lofty perch,
While whispering winds join in to lurch.
Each fluttering leaf holds a quip,
Nature's humor never does skip.

So let's raise a toast to all that's spry,
For every giggle as dark drifts by.
In afterglow where laughter reigns,
The world is dashed with fun refrains.

Photon Poetry

In beams of light, a comedy born,
Photons dance from dusk till morn.
Each flicker tells a tale anew,
Of jolly gnomes and dancing dew.

Optical pranks in a prism's glow,
Lead to laughter, oh what a show!
Sun rays tickle every creek,
Nature's voice, both bold and cheek.

A dazzling wink from the vibrant sun,
Makes critters giggle, oh what fun!
Each sparkle hums a silly tune,
As laughter blooms beneath the moon.

Join the chorus of light so bright,
Where every giggle sets worlds alight.
Photon tales flutter, twist, and soar,
Crafting joy forevermore.

Sun's Vibrant Voice

The sun awakes with a booming jest,
Tickling daisies, they stand at their best.
Giggling flowers, swaying with ease,
Chanting delight in every breeze.

Shadows wag their tails in glee,
As squirrels make fun of the old oak tree.
"Look at me!" they chirp and tease,
While sunlight dances, a playful breeze.

The horizon holds a bright confab,
Where laughter bursts like a bubbly tab.
All the critters can't help but grin,
Their joyful chorus a sweet violin.

So let the rays of merriment flow,
With each bright smile, the world will glow.
The sun's vibrant voice, a joyful decree,
Of laughter ringing, wild and free.

Daylight Testimonials

In the bright of day, we started to jest,
As shadows danced, boy did we quest!
With giggles and snickers, our tales came alive,
We laughed till we cried, oh what a drive!

Each anecdote spun, a stitch in our minds,
Of silly adventures and quirks that we find.
From aliens wearing socks to cats on a spree,
The daylight forgot to be dull, you see!

The sun played along, a cheeky little sprite,
As tales of the day turned into pure light.
With quirks so contagious, we rallied around,
In the warmth of our laughter, true joy was found!

So let's toast to the sun, with glasses held high,
To moments like these, we'll never say bye!
Each shout of delight, a bond freshly spun,
Our daylight testimonials, oh what fun we've begun!

Stellar Debates

We gathered 'round stars, with snacks piled high,
Debating whose comet could soar the most high.
With winks and some jabs, the cosmos our stage,
The laughter erupted, let's turn up the page!

A maestro made claims, his chin held with pride,
But a squirrel in space, he couldn't abide.
The moon chimed in too, with an echoing chortle,
As sunbeams aligned in a giggly mortal!

Galactic opinions tossed back like a game,
Who knew stars had rants, and were never the same?
There's a twinkle of wit in each orbiting turn,
And laughter ignites like a fiery burn!

So here's to the banter, the laughs and the cheer,
With stellar debates, we forget all our fear.
As we cheers with our cups, out past Pluto's gate,
To cosmic collisions that luckily translate!

Helios Chatter

The sun cracked a smile, oh what a delight!
We gathered at noon, basking in light.
With chatter so lively, we swayed with the breeze,
Each word a spark from the sun's playful tease.

A funny old fellow in flip-flops arrived,
He told of mishaps while having survived.
Like sunburned eyebrows and sandwiches stuck,
We giggled aloud, who knew we were so pluck!

There were tales of the heat that made shadows dance,
Of ice cream mishaps that led to romance!
Each moment a treasure, bursting in glee,
With smiles radiating, oh, how carefree!

So let's raise a cup and let laughter ignite,
With Helios' cheeky, sweet warm-hearted light.
As echoes of joy drift through skies up above,
We celebrate life with a sprinkle of love!

Dawn Sentiments

In the cradle of morn, we gathered with flair,
With yawns and some giggles, we danced in the air.
With sunlight that tickled our sleepy-eyed dreams,
We spun silly stories, all bursting at seams!

A rooster most chatty crowed tales like a king,
While pancakes flipped high, oh, the joy they'd bring!
With laughter like syrup drizzled with cheer,
Each moment we cherished, each chuckle sincere!

When the dawn started bright, with colors so bold,
We shared our life's secrets, now ready to unfold.
From socks that don't match to wild coffee spills,
In the warmth of our company, we banished the chills!

So here's to the dawn, its laughter, and light,
To memories we weave, so happy and bright!
With a wink and a smile, let's shout from our hearts,
In the glow of this morning, our laughter imparts!

Truths in Radiance

In a dance with rays that cling,
We juggle shadows, oh what a fling!
Truths are tickled in the gleam,
As laughter bubbles like a dream.

Witty whispers ride the beams,
Tickling thoughts like playful streams.
Each twinkle tells a silly tale,
While giggles glide without a fail.

Who knew a bright could be that bright?
Making mischief in the night.
With every flash, a chuckle shared,
A cosmic joke, and none are scared.

So bask in these absurd delights,
Where humor dances with the lights.
Embrace the truths that shine and play,
In laughter's glow, we drift away.

Light in the Lull

When the day takes a sleepy peek,
Light winks at us, oh so cheek!
Banter brews in the softest hue,
With giggles riding the sleepy dew.

In the hush, where twinkles tease,
They pull your leg with gentle ease.
Bright spirits spark a playful jest,
As silence whispers, "Aren't we blessed?"

Every beam has a story to tell,
In this cozy, giggling shell.
As the moon beams down some flair,
We chuckle under the silver glare.

So let's float on this drowsy light,
With silly puns that feel just right.
In the lull, where the fun won't cease,
We dance with laughter, finding peace.

Across the Solar Sea

On waves of glow, we skip and glide,
Through cosmic paths, our laughs collide.
Riding rays on a rubber raft,
Sunbeams chuckle, what a craft!

Bubbles pop with a silvery sound,
As we swirl in circles round and round.
Witty waves tickle our toes,
As dancing sparkles, oh how it glows!

Each splash a toast, a bright delight,
Making ripples in the night.
Silly moods in the solar sway,
We'll surf this joy, come what may.

Adventure calls on this shiny sea,
With laughter ringing, wild and free.
Together we float, in the gleeful spree,
Chasing happiness across, just you and me.

Leaping Lightframes

In frames of light, we leap and bound,
With jokes and jests, our hearts unbound.
Bright giggles turn the world to gold,
In the joyous tales we love to hold.

With every leap, a chuckle flies,
A symphony of fun in the skies.
We dance like shadows chasing sun,
In leaps of laughter, life's just begun.

Light plays tricks, like a clever mime,
Carving giggles, one frame at a time.
Each flicker is a playful tease,
We roll in laughter, oh what a breeze!

So let us leap through the glowing frame,
Each jump a spark, never the same.
In this realm of mirth and cheer,
We'll dance in light, forever near.

Radiating Revelations

A glow in the sky, oh what a sight,
Is it just me, or did that orb take flight?
With every wink, it brings a cheer,
Whispers of warmth, it holds so dear.

Elastic beams dance in the air,
Juggling giggles like they don't care.
Each ray a punchline, bright and bold,
Telling tales of laughter, yet untold.

Bouncing off rooftops, with flair galore,
Tickling the clouds, always wanting more.
Chasing the shadows, brightening faces,
Creating a symphony of silly graces.

As everyone basks in a golden glow,
One can't help but laugh, as they frolic below.
From dawn 'til dusk, let it be noted,
Laughter and joy are forever devoted.

A Daybreak Diary

A scribble of light upon the page,
It rises up, a giggly sage.
In the morning mist, with a sassy wink,
It spills stories before we think.

Pages of laughter, inked in glee,
Bouncing along like a bumblebee.
Each sentence giggles, each paragraph spins,
Sparks of humor, where the fun begins.

As the sun shows off in a playful way,
Judging no one, it's the life of the day.
Words prance around like they've won a race,
Leaving us tangled in a chuckle embrace.

So grab your pen, and let's not delay,
In this quirky novel, we'll laugh and play.
With every sunrise, let joy unfurl,
In the diary of light, we'll dance and twirl.

Celestial Chords

A strum of laughter from the sky,
Notes shimmer like stars as they fly.
Every chord tickles the cosmic air,
Melodies woven with whimsical flair.

Dancing along like a silly tune,
The sun joins in, a festive boon.
Whistling sweetly through cosmic spans,
In the orchestra of joy, it takes a stance.

Every dawn brings a brand new song,
With giggles bouncing where they belong.
In the symphony of life, bright and grand,
Together we sway in this sunlit band.

So let your heart join this quirky beat,
With every chord, life is such a treat.
In this concert of warmth and mirth,
Let's twirl in laughter, for all that it's worth.

Words Beneath the Surface

Hidden whispers beneath bright skies,
Where laughter bubbles and never dies.
With a wink, they rise like bubbly butter,
From the depths of giggles, no need to stutter.

Beneath the layers, where secrets lay,
A treasure trove of quips on display.
Each word is a nugget, shiny and bright,
Ready to burst into pure delight.

Eager to dance, they leap and spring,
Diving up high with a silly zing.
In this world of puns, we all take flight,
Trading our worries for sheer delight.

So let's unearth those gems of mirth,
And celebrate joy, for all that it's worth.
With every laugh and tune we unearth,
We cherish these moments, a joyful rebirth.

Stellar Soliloquy

In the cosmos, I lost my hat,
So I wore a pizza instead, how about that?
The stars giggle, dancing bright,
While I trip over rocks in the moonlight.

A comet told a joke, I could not catch,
It zoomed away, became quite a match.
The universe snickers at my clumsy glide,
And I wave at Venus, my cosmic guide.

Asteroids roll by, giving me the eye,
As I stutter and mumble, oh me, oh my!
They laugh at my shoelaces, one tied to a star,
Oh, cosmic blunders, how silly we are!

Jupiter joins in, with a belly so round,
While Saturn rings in, echoing the sound.
We chuckle together, under a sky so grand,
Creating humor across this starry band.

Eclipse of Expression

In shadows, I trip over my own two feet,
Turns out, moonlight is not so discreet.
I try to impress with my stellar moves,
But end up dancing like a car with no grooves.

A solar wink gave my ego a boost,
Yet my rhythm's more loopy than any space roost.
The planets watch, popcorn in hand,
As I attempt a spin, and fall in the sand.

Gravity giggles, pulling me down,
While stars make faces, why wear a crown?
I shout, "I'm a star!" as I stumble on air,
And moons roll their eyes, oh, they really don't care.

Uranus joins in with a cackle and whoop,
As I search for my dignity, lost in the scoop.
The universe laughs, its humor so grand,
While I just keep hopping, like a one-legged band.

Heatwave Musings

The sun decided to throw a roast,
While I attempted to butter my toast.
The solar flares toast me, oh how they glow,
But I'd rather dip fries in a cooler flow.

My brain sizzles like eggs in their shells,
As I look for shade and dodge pop-up wells.
The sidewalk shimmers, a wave of delight,
As I cartwheel past like a cartoon in flight.

Heat hitches a ride on my sweaty back,
While I juggle water, and dodge that quack.
A parched taco laughs, "You're one spicy dish!"
While I wish for ice cream, a cool, blissful wish.

So I doff my sunhat and dance like a clown,
Chasing the ice truck that rolls through the town.
The sun winks back, "What a sight to behold!"
As I scoff down cool treats, like treasure untold.

Luminous Reflections

Mirrors of starlight bounce off my nose,
While I try to invent some new cosmic prose.
I practiced my lines, not a single one hit,
So I scribble my thoughts on a galactic skit.

A black hole jokes, "You've got passion, my dear!"
As I float by like a quasar, filled with cheer.
Asteroids cheer me on, what a grand sight,
And I twirl in the darkness, a spark of pure light.

Nebulae giggle, in clouds of bright hue,
As I trip over stardust, there's laughter anew.
A space cat purrs, "You've got flair, it's true!"
While I drown in giggles from this cosmic crew.

So here I stand, a beacon of fun,
With laughter echoing, my joys weigh a ton.
In this universe large, with silliness low,
I bring forth the chuckles of life's cosmic show.

Resonating Rays

I told my friend a glowing tale,
He laughed so hard, he turned pale.
The sun was out, the jokes were bright,
We basked in jokes, a pure delight.

Then we spoke of twists and turns,
Of blazing truths that made us yearn.
Each quip a beam, each pun a flare,
In humor's warmth, we shed our care.

We danced around the midday heat,
With every line, the laughs repeat.
A radiant time, no shadows here,
Just smiles and giggles, full of cheer.

So come and join this sunny chat,
Bring your best joke, your fittest spat.
In radiant beams, we'll find our wits,
As laughter shines, the world just fits.

Heat-Drenched Narratives

In a land where summers blaze,
Tales emerge in fiery ways.
My cousin claims he caught a fish,
But it was mere a sunlit wish.

We laughed about his daring feat,
With every story, he felt the heat.
His wild claims and burning pride,
Had me rolling, tears I cried.

His tales of flames and great escapes,
Had us all drawing silly shapes.
With giggles bright and spirits bold,
Each jest a spark, a sight to behold.

On a sun-kissed day, we took our stand,
With punchlines scattered, oh so grand.
In heat-drenched tales, our hearts soared free,
Sharing laughter under the old maple tree.

Sunlit Solstice

Once at dawn, I sang a tune,
It was off-key, like a raccoon.
The sun arose, it rolled its eyes,
And chuckled bright 'neath azure skies.

My friend joined in with equal flair,
He hiccuped loud, oh what a pair!
We danced a jig, all out of sync,
With sunbeams laughing, what do you think?

Every tune a shining jest,
With rays of joy upon the quest.
In rhythm's chaos, we found our groove,
Sunlit giggles made us move.

So here we are, in golden light,
Creating joy, our hearts so bright.
With every laugh, a colorful spree,
On this solstice, we felt so free.

Brilliance in Brevity

In a fleeting glance, a smile was shared,
A joke so quick, the moment dared.
With wit so sharp, it cut right through,
And made the mundane feel brand new.

A single word, a punchline's spark,
In laughter's glow, we left our mark.
We danced on brevity's crisp embrace,
In quicksilver quips, we found our place.

A nodded laugh, a wink of glee,
In the blink of an eye, life's jubilee.
Each jest a firefly, bright and quick,
Lighting up the dark with every trick.

So cherish moments, fleeting and fun,
In brilliance caught, we all have won.
Each laugh a layer, a shimmering thread,
In the tapestry of words we've said.

Orbiting Echoes

In circles we chatter, like planets align,
With giggles that bounce, a delightful design.
Our jokes take the stage, like meteors bright,
As laughter ignites, in the shimmering night.

Around us they swirl, these tales we unfold,
Like comets on paths, both daring and bold.
In the cosmic ballet, where humor takes flight,
We orbit together, basking in light.

Radiance Unveiled

Peeking from shadows, a grin sure to shine,
With quirks and with quips, each twist is divine.
The universe giggles, as puns take their place,
A twinkle of wit, in this vast open space.

Bright beams of amusement, they dance and they play,
With each witty phrase, we chase clouds away.
In the gallery of stars, our humor's a gift,
Illuminating paths, giving spirits a lift.

Shadows of Brightness

In the nook of the night, where merriment fades,
We tickle the darkness, in whimsical parades.
The glimmer of laughter, it sparkles and sways,
Casting shadows of joy through the brightest of days.

Whispers of whimsy, they echo like stars,
Creating new worlds from the silliest bars.
With a punchline or two, we illuminate space,
In shadows of brightness, we find our place.

Light's Dialogue

When beams start to chat, their banter inspires,
With winks and with nods, they ignite gentle fires.
A conference of glows, with laughter at hand,
In the humor of light, together we stand.

As flashes engage, with each quirky jest,
They light up the room, putting smiles to the test.
With sparkling exchanges, so candid and warm,
In light's dialogue, we weather each storm.

Dazzling Monologues

In a crowded room, the spotlight gleams,
A jester's face, bursting with dreams.
Words tumble out in a gleeful race,
Who knew humor could wear such grace?

Each quip a rocket, soaring through air,
Laughter erupts, joining the fair.
Punchlines land like confetti rain,
Tickling ribs, easing all pain.

The crowd's a sea, waves of delight,
As one-liners dance into the night.
Jokes twinkle like stars on a clear eve,
In this galaxy, who dares to grieve?

With mischief in mind, the tales unfold,
Funny fables, both brave and bold.
A laughter storm, full of surprise,
Witty banter that never dies!

The Warmth of Words

Gather 'round, let me share a tale,
Of sunny thoughts that never pale.
Chuckle and snicker, let laughter flow,
As warmth ignites, and spirits grow.

Banter ignites like a summer breeze,
Ticklish whispers that aim to please.
Tongues as playful as a puppy's bark,
Finding joy in the quirks that spark.

I jest of socks and mismatched shoes,
And tell of squirrels with no sense of dues.
Every laugh a ray, shining so bright,
Chasing the clouds, inviting the light.

In this circus of chuckles, we all belong,
With every giggle, life's a song.
So let's revel in the absurdity here,
With humor as our guiding cheer!

Orbital Encounters

In a galaxy where humor flies,
Meteor jokes zoom through the skies.
Asteroids spinning, laughter rings,
Each laugh a planet, orbiting swings.

Comets blaze with tales outrageous,
Floating through space, quite contagious.
Stars wink and nod at the gags we spin,
Gravity's laughter pulls us all in.

From black holes to solar flares bright,
Jokes twist and turn in cosmic flight.
Alien antics, interstellar fun,
Our punchlines launch, we've just begun!

So join the ride, let's take to the sky,
With the universe laughing, oh me, oh my!
This orbit of joy will never cease,
In the vastness of space, we find our peace!

Zenith Musings

Atop the peak, where humor reigns,
Witty musings dance like trains.
Each thought a balloon, floating high,
Tickles like feathers that never die.

A summit of chuckles, laughter rings,
As we scribble jokes on paper wings.
High above, in the clear blue sky,
Punchlines leap and soar, oh my!

With each wisecrack, the view grows wide,
Life's quirks embraced, we take it in stride.
Silly banter fuels our ascent,
In this glorious giggle, we're all content.

So climb with me to this humorous height,
Where laughter echoes, day and night.
Our musings, a party, so rich and bright,
At the zenith of joy, everything's right!

Solar Serenade

In the sky so bright and bold,
Stars gossip tales, oh so old,
A wink from Mars, a chuckle from Venus,
As if the cosmos craves a genius.

Jupiter's storms dance like confetti,
While Saturn's rings are far too petty,
They laugh at Earth with coffee cups,
Galaxies gather, sharing hiccup ups.

A comet sneezes, oh what a sight!
And meteor showers light up the night.
The sun gives a nod, brewing up smiles,
While the moon hums softly, through cosmic miles.

So gather round, pull up a star,
Let's share our dreams, near and far,
With laughter swirling through the void,
In this solar dance, we're all overjoyed.

The Language of Light

A photon whispers, 'Hey, what's up?'
While electrons giggle, spilling their cup.
Quarks bounce around like kids at play,
Chatting in colors that brighten the day.

In the spectrum, they throw a big bash,
With lasers that mimic an interstellar flash.
Infrared joins with a wink and a grin,
While ultraviolet says, 'Let the fun begin!'

Each wave is a quip, each pulse, a jest,
In a dance where the light always knows best.
Photons are storytellers, bright and spry,
Sharing the mischief that flares in the sky.

The cosmos chuckles; it lights up the beat,
Fundamentals of joy, oh what a treat!
In this radiant party, we all play a part,
Speak the language of light straight from the heart.

Dappled Discourse

Twinkling glimmers in a cosmic chat,
Stars sharing secrets, imagine that!
They twirl and twist in dappled delight,
Crafting charm in the velvety night.

Nebulas whip up a folklore stew,
While black holes just wink, 'We know the view!'
Supernovas burst, what a fabulous scene,
As laughter echoes from realms unseen.

Planets pull pranks, it's a galactic game,
Venus slips on a space-time frame.
The Milky Way giggles, a cosmic jest,
As comets streak by in their fiery vest.

Quasars chuckle, their beams in a spin,
A chorus of laughter, a light-hearted din.
Join in the fun, feel the starlit embrace,
In this dappled discourse, we find our place.

Galactic Revelations

In the depths of space, laughter resounds,
With planets that joke 'round cosmic bounds.
Pulsars tick-tock like clocks gone wild,
While the universe plays, just like a child.

Stars spin yarns in a twinkling race,
While black holes smirk at a cosmic chase.
Asteroids tumble, drop puns on the way,
Throwing stardust jokes every light year's play.

Gravity giggles, pulling us near,
As starlight shimmers, dispelling all fear.
Galaxies whirl, in a brilliant ballet,
Whispering tomfoolery in their own way.

So tune in to the laughter up high,
A cosmic comedy, let spirits fly!
In this grand tapestry, humor does reign,
With galactic revelations, joy is our gain.

Bright Futures Unspoken

In the sky, we chase the glow,
While hats fly off in the sun's warm show.
A squirrel pauses, dines on some cheese,
Pretending it's royalty, oh what a tease.

Balloons escape from sticky hands,
While laughter dances across the lands.
We plot our dreams with giggles and cheers,
Hoping they sprout like bright balloons through years.

Ice cream melts on an eager tongue,
As jokes are told and songs are sung.
Every hiccup, a cause for delight,
In this bright world, everything feels right.

So here's to the moments of giddy delight,
With shadows that play and sunlight so bright.
We'll wave to the clouds and chase down the fun,
For life is a party, and we've just begun.

Dancing with Daylight

Over the hills, our shadows prance,
As if they know we're in a dance.
The sun winks down, a playful tease,
While we spin around among the trees.

The grass tickles toes like a feather's soft brush,
As giggles erupt in a carefree hush.
We've lost our shoes in the adoring dirt,
These little adventures, our hearts they convert.

In a world where giggles are currency gold,
Every tickle fight is a treasure untold.
With a leap and a bound, we challenge the sun,
To chase us forever, a race just for fun.

By twilight's embrace, the laughter won't cease,
For daylight's ballet brings nothing but peace.
We bow to the stars, our joy takes its flight,
Dancing with daylight till we bid it goodnight.

Reflection of the Stars

When the night falls, the giggles ignite,
Reflecting on dreams, we soar into flight.
With wishes like fireworks, we scribble our fate,
And the moon chuckles softly, isn't it great?

We bounce on the lawn, like and round merry-go-rounds,
While crickets play tunes with their rhythmic sounds.
A comet zooms by, wearing a wink,
As we sip on lemonade and spill every ink.

The stars are our audience, twinkling so bright,
As we strut like we're actors, taking the night.
Our laughter is louder than any grand show,
Creating constellations of joy that just flow.

So here's to reflections, our giggles in tow,
Under galaxies sparkling, like a grand light show.
With stardust on fingers, we scribble away,
In the galaxy of laughter, forever we'll play.

Secrets of the Solar Wind

The wind whispers secrets, all giggles and cheer,
As it tickles our faces, bringing joy near.
We chase it around, like butterflies fly,
With a hop and a skip, we dance under the sky.

The clouds hold the laughter, soft and aloof,
As we bounce on the grass, letting out a woof.
The sun plays peek-a-boo, a mischievous friend,
Its rays turning puddles to laughter that blend.

Little green aliens join in the fun,
With goofy green hats, they dance 'til they're done.
In this whimsical world, we twirl with delight,
As cosmic balloons float away into night.

So here's to the secrets the solar winds bring,
Our laughter and joy, the wildest of things.
With whimsy and wonder wrapped tight in our hands,
We'll play in this universe, no limits, no plans.